Mind Lesions

A collection of Poetry

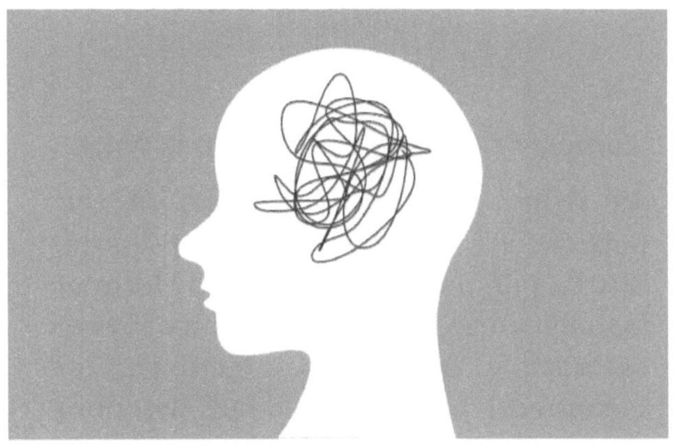

By

M. Hutman & D.B. Wright

Cover art by SueAnn Summers Griessler

Paperback ISBN: 978-1-9168779-1-7

Published by D.B. Wright Publishing, U.K

DEDICATION

This book is dedicated to each other and to all the fellow survivors, dreamers and believers.

AUTHOR FOREWORD BY D.B. WRIGHT

There are moments in a writer's life that help define their journey. One such moment for me was connecting with Mia, who was an established writer in the online scene when I first dipped my foot in the water in 2020. She was one of the writers that I immediately looked up to for her fearless and free style of writing and her obvious passion for the artform of words.

I first had the honour of collaborating with Mia in December of 2020, after which we became close friends and constant collaborators. There is something about how our two minds operate together that just seems to work, without pressure or effort. Writing together is so natural and free, and we allow each other to go to any place our minds take us, without fear of judgment.

For me, this book is an expression of the connection we have made as humans and as writers. It also symbolises a pivotal moment in my writing journey, in both meeting and collaborating with this incredibly talented yet humble human being. Long may we be friends and collaborators.

D.B. Wright (Danny Boy)

AUTHOR FOREWORD BY M. HUTMAN

I put my dreams on hold many times for many people in my life: choosing to do so changed me as an individual. Putting others before myself made me question who I was as an individual: who was I without labels and boxes checked off on a questionnaire? Losing my sense of self brought me back to writing. Experiencing long lasting trauma, made me find my voice and I no longer wanted to be silenced.
I chose to share online as an act of healing myself, purging, and I jumped in with both feet. I passionately gave myself to my craft. I let go without worry of judgement in the online community.

My muse was myself. I was searching to heal the old me and come out anew. I very rarely shared my words with anyone outside of the online community. Having the support and friendship of Danny has altered my life and my thoughts. I don't feel alone anymore as Danny is someone who didn't judge me based on my past or present circumstances. He understood me through my poetry. He held space for me when the waves of darkness came. He has always let me be myself and we easily connected our words to create many collaborations.

This book is a collaboration of our soul spills, our friendship and our desire to heal from wounds that take so much longer to mend.

m. hutman (Mia)

FOREWORD FROM STUTI SINHA

I have known Danny as a writer since 2020 and when I think about how his word and craft has evolved in the last year, I am reminded of a quote by Peggy Noonan which reads -

"Part of courage is simple consistency"

I can't think of many people who demonstrate as much courage as Danny does. And courage isn't a muscle that he only flexes as a creator or an artist. Courage is one of the pillars of who Danny is as a human being. It therefore automatically reflects, in both his writing and approach to it.

His range as a writer spans across a broad spectrum of subjects like love, sensuality, internal reflection, grief, trauma, and mental health. He doesn't flinch from serving his honest opinion, experience, and point of view through his art; nor does he soften the sensory impact of those (maybe difficult) experiences.

"Everything sits heavy, like unspent bullets In sniper pockets.
Every breath like adding vinegar to sunburnt skin.
Each thought salts the wounds of the one before it.
A wooden puppet of my inner child sits on my stomach,

drumming on my chest: pulverising my pleural cavity with the same old beats of near-death defeat."

These opening lines of his piece 'Tomorrow Sorrow' are testament, to Danny's unshrinking honesty as a writer. He doesn't hold back or dodge around expression. He just expresses with a sharpness and intensity that is inimitable. You will laugh, and shed tears, and forget to breathe or gasp and swell with love and bleed and go through an emotional experience in pages. Even when subjects and human experiences may be completely unknown to you; Danny's writing will make you feel.

And this is a person who doesn't just communicate his first-hand experience and feelings but has the INCREDIBLE ability to slip into characters and to feel and write from their perspective.
'A Thousand Times' is an example of exactly that:

"I can cause pain that stays for decades
And you'll still thank me,
For what I give, you gladly receive;
Still worship me (with monied prayer)
In the twisted altars of your psyche.
I can be the bitch you wish the sweet ones would be.
The whore they can't even imagine,
And match their innocent smiles while I do it."

It is this versatility and ability to slip into characters that makes Danny a treat to co-write with. He shares this gift of collaborative work with readers on his digital platforms. His generosity makes way for seamless creative blending with others in which both his own, and the co-writers' work shines.

Mia and his writing matched together presents a unique gift to readers. Mia has an extraordinary command of language. She is unapologetic yet tender in her expression, abandoned yet evocative, fiery when she wills, and vulnerable when she needs to be. Together they connect on subjects that they both have intense familiarity with. And their passion to write on those subjects, laced with their unique styles is unparalleled. Their collaborations are testament to their transcendent connection which offers an experience; one that I believe no reader of modern prose and poetry should be denied of.

Stuti Sinha – Poet & Author

FOREWORD FROM EMILY WILLARD

I stumbled across Mia and her poetry whilst watching an Instagram live just under a year ago and I was instantly enamoured by her words. The fearlessness and power I felt in just the one piece of prose exuded so much strength and truth I knew I just needed to know more about her; finding myself lost in a maelstrom of deep, raw unfettered emotion with every poem I read.

There is no doubt that when EXPERIENCING her words you as a reader are going to feel.

I say experience because It almost feels like Mia breaks open her ribcage, and pulls a pen straight from her heart. She bleeds emotion and life experience unapologetically from brain to page. I am reminded of this quote by the author Natalie Goldberg.

"Write what disturbs you, what you fear, what you have not been willing to speak about. Be willing to be split open."

That is exactly what Mia does. She splits herself open for her art. Mia has a voice and a lens that clearly belongs to only her, and she is not afraid to use it, crafting magick in the form of poetry and prose.

Without shying away from anything in her writing, the transparency she offers readers makes the content of her poetry so much more tangible, and even uncomfortable at times. She has an ability to access her life experience, and turn it into art, doing so with such fierce bravery you cannot help but be moved by her expression.

"Dear Lord God Jesus, if you can hear me: my name is Mia. I am seven years old. Can you please take away my insatiable pain? I am a good girl. I think he is a bad man. Amen"

In the piece 'Repent' she portrays a painful vulnerability by walking us into her world allowing us to be part of her human experience from child to adult.

When reading Mia and Danny's collaborations, there are moments where, as a reader, you are shook to your core by what you have just read. It's almost as if someone has crawled under your skin, grabbed you by the bones and rattled you around a bit. Words gain a whole new life and layer when they blend their minds together, thereby offering to their readers an experience which you are bound to live in as you turn the pages.

Emily Willard – Poet and Author

CONTENTS

from the soul of Mia

from the soul of Danny

from both souls

ACKNOWLEDGMENTS

Together, we would like to acknowledge:
Soul Connection Poets
Our amazing cover artist, SueAnn
Suti and Emily for writing Forewords

Mia would like to personally acknowledge:
All the beautiful souls that I have melded in genuine connection with, support, laughter, tears, understanding, forgiveness and a love that transcends words.

Danny would like to personally acknowledge:
The Literary Pages Assembly
Glass of Mead
My writer friends and peers; so many great connections out there.

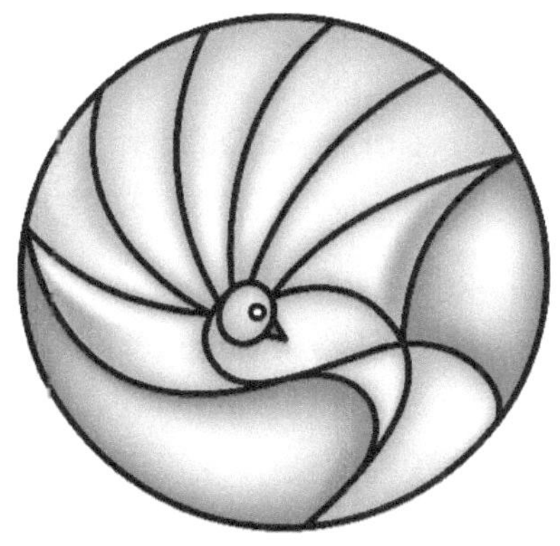

FROM THE SOUL OF MIA

This section contains solo poetry by myself, Mia (m.hutman). These selected poems are personal to my journey, my choices, my mistakes, my deaths and the growth of who I am today. It speaks to my bent limbs, battered contusions and my resiliency to never quit on myself.

"If I got rid of my demons,
I'd lose my angels."
- Tennessee Williams

diaphanous eyelids

I see you on the back of my eyelids when I pretend I am sleeping but actually I am just slowing dying inside:

filling myself up with the darkness that only comes out at night, by surprise: it chokes my light and dismembers my limbs before I can decide to runaway from this guttural inhabitant that pretends to love me for me

you are screaming out my name and these walls are closing in around my pounding temples and I try to fuck myself free but I only am hurting myself more by not swallowing the real trauma: being dissociative is best served in a gushing fucking mess

I feel you leaking out of my teardrops and I try to stop myself from overthinking, overreacting, overdosing in the pain that is me missing you from every inch of my skin: my heart is exhausted and I don't know how to end back up in your arms

maybe I didn't try hard enough to save you that night: maybe I was the one that was supposed to die splattered on the pavement but god is playing a joke on me like she always does since the beginning of my lost childhood innocence: I am nothing to her, I am nothing that she remembers because it's been so many years and I never pray to her invisibility

maybe loosing you is my punishment for never being good enough for anyone who has tried to love me but I fail them on repeat

I run up and down these streets in a daze: getting lost in skylines, architecture and the smell of the sea

If I scream at the top of my lungs would you hear me in heaven

If I whisper I miss you will you show up when I finally open my eyes again.

I run up and down these streets in a daze: getting lost in

I am all the things you deny exist within yourself.
I am all things you're scared to see
when you avoid self reflection.
You are waves of resistance.

There's no poem in me today

there is no poem in me today
just a lump in my throat
yeah it hurts but I am used to it
I am unable to swallow
and I wish you were here
with your hands
firmly placed around my neck
feeding me
driving your pain into me
making me forget who I am
coating me in ways
that make the world end
and nothing matters
but our atoms
our storms
our concave bodies
falling
f a l l i n g
f
a
l
l
i
n
g
in rhythmic wayside
where we're just sweat
hunger
nectar
bites
swallowed bliss
and the world

fades to grey
we paint each other
happy
and laugh till it
hurts so good
we make love
till we're embedded
in the other's dream

there is no poem in me today
just this heavy ton weight
sitting on my chest
the scalpel doesn't get deep
e n o u g h
never enough
I dig myself out
but still
I am not hallowed
doctor says I need
a pacemaker
I say she needs to change
her meds
and quit cheating on her husband
he already knows
and doesn't have the balls
to confront her
she doesn't like my honesty
and I clearly don't give a fxck
actually I care too much
and now here I am
laying
bare breasted
nipples to the ceiling
waiting for an uneducated

answer to why
my heart
is no longer mine
I don't know what zipcode
she has laid her head in
who's chest she has
s u n k into
I hope he holds her
gently
memorizing her curvature
I hope he cares and listens
I hope he loves her laugh lines
I hope he is in a good place
I hope my wishes don't fall
on deaf ears
I hope he teaches
her
how to find
her way
back home
when he's done with her.

Him.

(him)
death speaks to you between sunsets
and that's the time you run away from me because you
don't feel comfortable showing me your demons but I chase
you down and show you who is in control

(me)
you tattoo my pain in thunder and rain: leaving me
abandoned in a cold wet bed before you tie me up and
punish me for not accepting your slippery hands across my
face

(him)
weeping willows weave stitches in my skin: you are my
favorite nurse
you heal me with your love: needle, thread and steady
hands as you always fix this brokenness inside of me and I
cannot wait to thank you by grabbing you by the throat

(me)
my stain glassed bones shatter under each one of your
blows but down the rabbit hole I go for that's the only place
where you won't follow: through the looking glass I don't
see hope and I don't feel fear

I have erased you from your almost home, almost baby,
almost fairytale love, almost dreams of forever

I don't feel you in my flesh and blood
I have purged you from my mouth, my womb, my heart, my
soul, my mind

In my nightmares you still haunt me,
rape me, tell me you love me and you
come up behind me and choke me out
till I wake up drenched in my own sweat: alone in my
fucking king size bed that you've never touched
In my nightmares you make me your servant your
concubine your bride
I am chained to wrist and you don't allow me to speak to
think or drink
In my nightmares I push you down an empty well and watch
you cry for forgiveness from your mental hell
I sit on the edge and wonder why I ever believed you were
the one who could save me: when you only ever made me
feel dead

All there ever was, was:
asphyxiated privation.

25

No hearsay: biting my tongue
and your secrets I swallowed.

the importance of breaking people

I. I heard god calling my name but I drove my car into a tree because the skeletons were too heavy: they beat down my heart's door and made me watch myself be raped again

II. The pain is inevitable and all I want to do is jump till my neck breaks: stop my breathing and drain me of my baptism because my church is within

III. The world is better backwards so I step on all the cracks to break my mother's back: she doesn't feel a thing she's too busy ignoring me so I let her think she wins

IV. The needle and thread have retired for the night: too tired to sew my drawn out dislocated wounds, they sleep with the angels while my splintered skinsuit scales prick up at the thought of drowning at sea

V. The importance of breaking me open is the same as giving birth to a stillborn and waiting to hear god laugh in your face when it's discarded by the staff

deleted hard drive

//the things I've deleted//

now I lay me cown to sleep
but you strangulate me
now I lay in a crumpled mess
on these sheets of forced
ticking time bomb clocks
upon my swollen lips
you lay your head
your demons are afraid of me
I am but a child
and still you seek me
you don't repent your wickedness
on your deathbed
I laughed out loud
I was but 11
//
now I drown in the blackness
of your bath water
no evidence on my skinsuit
everything remains buried within
the bullets smell intoxicating
the gun on your nightstand loaded
but your sea eyes haunt me
as you watch me scrub myself raw
and you talk to me about tomorrow
I know I'll never see you
I've wished you dead 1000 times

in the last 120 minutes alone
//
now I delete my memory bank
I am not a crumbled mess of:
rubble, wilted petals, cornered book pages unread
and screaming silent nightmares
I heal
I heal
I heal
I delete the hard drive
I delete the sound of your existence
I set fire to everything that I've ever known
I am made anew and your bones lay in the soil
where my sunflowers grow.

Yesterday:
bellow my name as I deposit you in my back pocket.

Hope ties its noose around my neck:
I refuse to jump.

the boogeyman

I'm the boogeyman that haunts your head
I pull you by your hair and tell you what a fucking mess you
are: nothing but a disappointment as I slap your cheeks
pink red purple and blue; limbs severed and you still try to
hold onto me like your favorite pounded bleeding treasure:
oh how I love the taste of you

You spit your saliva into my mouth and make me
bite off the tip of my tongue: telling me to recognize my
wickedness because I deserve to suffer when you are in
excruciating pain: when you are at war with yourself; I must
support you and be chaos to your schizophrenic thoughts

I'm the boogeyman that haunts your head
I nail you down to the hardwood floors and fuck my steel
into your peony till you bleed and cry for me to love you:
I'm the best you've ever had and my name leaves your lips
of bliss as I mark you as my prophecy

You cut me down with the sharpest blade and let me bleed
out at the torii gates
you don't look back: you have no remorse
you take yourself to the sea and shed your skinsuit:
coming out renewed and vindicated
you now have erased your boogeyman status and are just
the prince charming I first fell in love with

I drop to my knees and I apologize for making you rape me,

making you hit me, making you choke, making you posses
me
You forgive me and I love you again as only I can: next week
we begin again and the boogeyman eats my guts and my
brains

Depression makes me call out to you
in dreams that I lay awake for.

dearly departed

dearly departed I've been fucking dead inside since the age
of seven: this fake smile washed away by tears and this
guttural churning turning fear
I walk in circles: ring around the rosies pocket full of rocks in
this broken heart
my dress full of posies but you are just staring at my pussy
like the sick fuck that you are
I want to cut you up and feed you to my pigs

dearly discarded what the fuck is wrong with me
what the fuck is wrong with you
what the fuck does this even mean
I don't give a fuck what you think of me
I don't give a fuck if I am lovable
at least I am fucking kind and I don't do to you what you
have done to me

dearly abandoned I am hanging myself on every word that
tries to break my neck
I don't want to fucking die: I want to fucking live my life
without the nightmare of my avatar dying in my other sims
game Truman Show shit show cloud atlas slipstream life
let me learn to be happy without the fear that everyone and
everything will be deleted from my memory bank and I
must start over this 8 minute game called life.

35

My saltwater tears
rice old wounds
as you silently watch me.

the webs we weave

the webs we weave to unfuck ourselves from purgatory's
throat
orb weaver deceiver not keen on telling truths
but halfass sticky diluted proofs
tell me lies
tell me lies
tell me sweet honey
dripping from your mouth
l i e s
I lick your face
because you taught me how to love the hurt
when I leave you: I don't even look back
at the ghost of you

the webs we weave to unstitch our constricting threads: we
hide our villains in ugly sweaters and wear our hearts on our
sleeves just to be left on the street like an overlooked
homeless begging for forgiveness and a sandwich from an
imaginary god we all wait on for saving.

glasshouse depression

I try to rip you out of my throat. You know my first name but I'll never take your last. I'm so fucking sick and tired of swallowing you down. What a bitter tasting reminder you are. The caffeine is not strong enough today and you taste like cigarettes and the suicide note I wrote when I was seven. I'm the villain in every story and you're always the lovable rapist cf my soul. I don't give a fuck what you think of me anymore. The sky is so pink and bubblegum blue in the driveway where I am keeled over: my fist are tight and my chest tighter. The sun is hitting my lungs and I learn to breathe again. Cough the smoke out and blink away two tears. I get in my car and runaway. No map or destination will ever take me away from your grasp. I don't understand why you feel like I need you to hold my hand while chocking my existence. I don't love you and you don't love me. Our love affair is toxic. I will never marry you. I am exhausted and want you out of my bloodstream. I need you to quit screaming in my ear because I don't give a fuck about your needs: all you do is throw me inside your coffin and bury me with your fake-ass preaching verses. You want me to tongue kiss death as you jerk off in the corner of the room: inside our purgatory glass house. I am sorry to tell you but I have decided to put myself first. I take the ax to your throat because killing me is the only way to kill you too. I'm going to watch you take your last breath: then I'll get on my knees and pray to myself.

me. just me

The ground is saturated with the stillness of orange leaves that have mistakenly erased my missing and mourning. open underlined pages are fast to take hold of random gusts of blowing air cycles. the old me dead and gone: just bones tied to an ash. the sky has vanished entirely from my eyes as my dreams are drawn out of dust and my fingerprints have been sanded off each hand. the ringing in my ears is so uncomprehendingly funneled down the curve of my neck that I cannot hear a damn thing. fucking goosebumps sprawl themselves across my skin and laugh at my jokes. I expected autumn to shed my darkness but she only lapped at my shores with an insatiable thirst for my truth. I am looking in the mirror for the answers to spill out of my soul but I fear I have lost all sense of control. the world is noir and I am eating bullets to taste the love you ripped out of me. I ask myself: who are you now? I ask the gods the same question but I get no response as they have refused to acknowledge my existence.

39

Wet waves washing wounds worthy of wordless worries.

I blanket my bareness, for you cannot feel me or see me anymore. You told me my skin is too rough: too many scars to run the palms of your hands over.

repent

I am going to paint your mouth shut till you no longer
salivate. If you speak out of turn I'm going to stick my hand
down your thorax and rip out your voice box. You are a child
of the good book: go to bed and repent your sins. Neon
prayers fell from my childish pout:

Dear Lord God Jesus, if you can hear me: my name is Mia. I
am seven years old. Can you please take away my insatiable
pain? I am a good girl. I think he is a bad man. Amen

I am in love with standing on the gravel before the train is
on it's way down the tracks. I feel the rush on my face. The
anticipation does something to my guts. I open my mouth
to scream but I am weak: voicebox dejected. The force of
the train knocks me down the hill. I am bruised and bleeding
but on the inside I am already numb and don't know how to
cry anymore.

I go home, put my childish hands together; on my knees I
repent my sins.

Dear Lord God Jesus, if you are listening: my name is Mia. I
am eight years old. Can you grant me one wish? Take me
away. I don't fit in here and he doesn't fit inside of me
either. I am a good girl. I think he is a bad man. Can you let
me die please? Amen

I am in love with drowning because I am a weak swimmer;
never taught by my parents. I jump into the river and let it
fight me with closed fist. I don't go under and

disappointment seeps into every one of my heart valves. The river now my only best friend and she hugs me so fucking tightly that I puke her out. I try to scream at her for not allowing me to join her in her depths. She told me she loves me and that's when I knew she was the best mom I have ever had.

Neon prayers are stuck in my throat. I pray for the last time in my life.

Dear Lord Jesus, I know you are not there for me. You don't watch over me. You are clearly busy with other more important children. My name is Mia. I am nine years old. Can you kill him? I am a good girl. He is The Bad Man. Am I joke to you? Why have you not granted my wish? I will never ask for anything again. You can take away all my dolls and toys but please kill him: he is hurting me. Amen

I am in love with myself. Neon prayers are dead and gone. My voice box restored. My last wish granted.

Featherweight paper hearts torn in the catching wind:
never whispering apologies

Denumbed within my noise:
silent eternal voicebox dejected.

Diaphanous mazarine painted skies:
your soul weeping noir charcoal raindrops down my thorax.

death is a woman

the sea stretched out of its shell, as she broke open and shed herself onto the sands of time that forgave her for accepting all of your closed fist mistakes. the waves told her how you never loved her and how she was never tied to you by rings or vows: she leaned into loss and mourned every liquid she shed to keep you from falling out of her. the window is open and she let you leave her sweet abode. you are not welcome to ever return. she is exhausted of re-living the death of you, your fists, you rapping every inch of her. her atoms are puking you out on the side of the highway and her brain is tired of you chasing her through her nightmares.

death is a woman who doesn't belong to anyone. she has metal bones and gasoline blood: she doesn't need to be loved by your angels or demons. she sets herself on fire to escape your grip from her throat. she drips pain onto pages and licks it off the blade before she plunges it back in.

death is a woman who will never beg to be saved by the likes of you. she is a hurricane prone to desolate cities that have known her shoreside. she has been nothing but a good giver, a love letter, a muse, and a story you'll tell your friends when you are shitfaced. death will drop kick you off a cliff and tell you to swim because she knows you love shallow and lack patience for depth.

death is a woman who is cursed by the stars to lose her gods and all she knows how to do is suffer alone. she is a tug of war in all her lifetimes: her tongue spits the venom from the ones who pretended to love her for her. there's a story and storm brewing, but you'll never be invited inside of her.

I swallow our entanglement whole:
you waterboarding your love into me.

certain death

Before this certain death I chose to watch my life pass me by on storytelling storm clouds that embraced all my demons. They held me by the hand and led me in the right direction but I was full of resistance and built a wall around my anatomical clock heart. Pacemaker is what the cardiologist predicted with his magic 8 ball, pearly bite and soft hand stethoscope on my chest. I told him I will not be a slave to my heart (condition) but he just said I was a stubborn beautiful soul. I told him I would never bite my tongue and I always swallow. Here's a prescription to heal the death of your heart from the age of seven he signed into his pad. I wanted nothing more than to jump feet first into the void of my favorite drug: myself. I couldn't let go as I wanted to. I couldn't breathe while running so far away from my exhausted darkness. I couldn't breathe while insomnia inseminated me with convulsions and convictions that I was in the wrong. I couldn't breathe when I told someone I loved them but I was barren in a mirage of illusions that they were never mine. There was no fear inside of me but somehow I betrayed myself on some days when I wasn't gentle with my inner child. She didn't cry for her abandonment, her molestation, her rapes, her abuse, her homelessness or the violence her bones took to heal from repeatedly. I may not know much but I know that loving myself with both arms is the only thing I can depend on. I will not be blinded by my flaws or weaknesses for denial is not in my blood stream any month of the year.

a witch

enters your heart to hold you the way you need it but are
too scared to admit it//enters your heart and galvanizes
your aches till you know you are safe

kisses your deep seated wounds and sits with you in
darkness without a single word on her tongue//blows
healing into your picked at scabs till you are sutured with
infinite love fluid

enters your soul and continuously drips her faith into all
your porous cavities: expanding in girth till you are full of
her unconditional devotion//she believes in you
wholeheartedly and breaths to show you

tells you the stories from long ago, where you each were
one combined soul//she wipes your tears after amnesia has
disappeared and knowing has set in

enters your mindscape with gentle pressure, she doesn't
change your thinking but inserts her seed into you: watering
you for growth and reminding you of your worthiness to be
loved//she matches your thoughts, your verbal, your
throats longing, your need, your understanding: she puts
her dreams into you long before you have them

she is light//she is dark
she is the embodiment of the divine
she is the giver//she is the taker

she is everything your lungs require
she is everything you ache for
she is the only lover you desire
she is loyal//she is unselfish
she is the one you live for
she is the one you die beside

shadow

turn your back on me like you always have. even your shadow walks away from me and I grow cold in a universe made for me by me that you take free will out of. I crave warmth and a blanket but you abandon me at their doorstep. vengeance is the rusty key you hold against my lips. pride is what you beat into my chest as he rapes me and calls me his submissive bride of christ. anger lava you've poured into my eyes to blind me to the truth. feeding me lies with a silver spoon kneeling on a pew. take of my body: drink of my blood while in my head I've killed you a million times. I take the blade out of it's sheath and behead you for your sins. I don't repent a goddamn thing because I am not to blame. pulling the arrows from my Being because I don't feel pain anymore. you took everything away from me, starting at the age of seven. I never cried: I fucking hate you. now I know not to have faith in imaginary holograms. your shadow can smite me but I don't believe anything you say because you are silent: dormant: dead from my blade.

the feeding upon

Once upon a time, the clocks stopped, and I didn't have to run away from the adults with wolf eyes and insatiable bites.

alphabetical moments

I had my legs dangling over the edge of the bridge that mid-afternoon. My sandals sat next to me and my earbuds were pounding music into my prefrontal cortex. My lips synchronized to the lyrics and my eyes slowly closing, as I became one with the song. I released the tension from my shoulders: leaning into the steel of the bridge, as my breast pressed themselves into the coldness. I had the warmth of the sun beating down from above: my thoughts spilling themselves into the rhythm of the breeze. The moment was all my own. Inevitable erosion of my thoughts splattered across watercolour skies. I had come to my favourite spot just to get away from it all: to find within myself that place that needed to be shocked back to the realization that my sadness was black and beaming. The colour of my love a shade of noir without a name. Destination unknown. Self-destruction imminent again. I didn't deny the pain I was experiencing, but I was all alone in the world with your bloodstream kiss still stuck to my lips. I took the shallowest breath and the dead calm washed itself over me in a swift icy fear dipped paint brush. I became voiceless: a selective mutism in my mouth. Ripping my words into alphabetically deranged moments of when you weren't dying, we weren't star crossed and I didn't feel so out of place. I was eternally dreaming of you, but reality always gutted me and I knew I'd walk back home without you ever being there waiting for me.

note to self

I fell so hard onto the concrete, that my knees scraped the gravel and I had not yet felt the blood trickling down my legs. I let out a sigh with the wind slapping my flushed cheeks. I have come to the conclusion that I have fallen for the dead parts of you. I am patient and don't dare ask you to skip to the good parts where forever is just a second longer than the last time I held you.

monster

I Believe you are a monster:
here to tear out my wings every chance you get. Plucking each individual one out, slowly with precise accuracy for your morose satisfaction. You want to make me pay for your unhappiness, your guilt, your devoided voice, but all you're left with is unanswered prayers from your god. He doesn't listen to you, for you are not his child: just a spawn, a jaw dropping knees bent on a filth pew, child of egotistical proportions.

I Believe you are a monster who doesn't know what love is at all. You've never been born: you've never been birthed out of it's canal. You've never been held just to experience it's overwhelming power take control of your entire Being. You don't know how to give love, as you've never had it put inside of your life force. You cannot keep pretending to be the victim of this sick reality that you've created and called it: home sweet home, hush your mouth don't tell anyone, don't embarrass the family name. You don't know the definition of love. You don't know it's value. You don't know how to give it freely to your children. Love to you constitutes this picture perfect, 2 doctors family, white picket fence mentality where everyone is a barcode consumer zombie of the good book.

I Believe you are a monster for trying to ignore, delete, cut out my trauma to keep up with appearances. You've abandoned me decades ago. You've tried to delete my voice from your psyche many years ago so you can sleep better knowing you didn't protect me. You will never get a chance to rip out my voice box because it will just regenerate like an octopus limbs. I will never listen to you, because I am

Rebellious. In my rebellion I am free and I am nothing like you. What a gift that is to my healing and my children. You will never know what love is, even if YOU were the one being molested with it as a child and not ME.

winter tastings

winter tastes like a stalemate and the moulding eggnog forgotten inside the kitchen sink but you my love taste like the Bermuda triangle: wet on my tongue;
a disappearing act of false faith as I fall deeper, never to return again because winter only brings death and making love in front of the fireplace while it snows outside our windows: our limbs entanglements of all our past lives

winter tastes like an ashtray and sweat dripping down every inch: beneath each breast lay the shrapnel you left embedded as a reminder that you had me once and made me believe that spring would never come: such a comedy are you: such a tragedy to think I once believed in all seasons: I once believed in you

winter taste like me tasting me off of your fingers and that Dutch apple pie recipe you know how to make from memory as I sit naked on the kitchen counter watching you in your element and you sing me songs and make laugh out loud till it hurts and you kiss me like we're actually in love with each other and not the people in our heads

winter tastes like forbidden fruit dripping from my mouth as you lick my face but we both know you are no god to me just a mortal with a huge agenda to muddy my dawn as I am a lotus and you are my grave robber.

Things That Don't Suck
(1) being seen
(2) being heard
(3) being felt
(4) being loved
(5) being held

who is god?

who is god but seven shades of sadness seeping sorrows
slowly into sweet sanguine slumbering sleep until soft
saturated silk snakes shake you awake with slithering
salubrious strangulated
salvation from strangers?

who is god but deluged dreams drawn out of dust dripping
down desolate doorways denouncing dented delusions of
demoralizing destruction departing deplorable
decomposing bones?

who is god but a poet peeling parts of you out of your
poems: protesting proverbs and painting punctured
punctuation piled into putrefaction of paradoxical
paradigms particular to petrified petroglyphs of your
unfolding life?

get off your knees or stay there but the outcome is the
same: free will is the liar in your soul.

dear m,

who are those who suffer?
I do not know, but they are my people.

loneliness begins the climb up the riverbed: we do not rest
against organized devil webs. we make our way down the
mountain, humming a reverberating tune.

it is much too heavy to carry such a burden: we stand up &
we are surrounded by the sweetest breeze. my thoughts try
to find quietude against my cracked sternum.

anxiety throws her hat to the psithorism and it picks up the
hem of my summer dress: I begin to twirl in the field
revealing all the scars you've cut so deep into me. left to
fend for myself and that's how I knew to never depend on
anyone since childhood.

I tell her that I don't think of him in my daily hustle, but in
the darkroom of night he crawls under my covers and begin
to take from me everything I've worked so hard to keep.
such a haunting rapist is he.

I tell her: let's go: you, me, and the hidden intimacy that no
one sees till I let them love the bones of me: till I let them
devour me wholly and I love them unconditionally for who
they are and not their potential.

next to me she has wild eyes and in the midst she sees the
world differently than most: never scared, but butterflies
distract her from being cautious: her battles fought alone
and understanding is not something easily found in another.

she takes my hand and puts it to my chest: she doesn't want
me to let the blood leak out of my sleep. she tells me the
train is leaving with or without me: am I staying in the
hungering grief or do I step into the fire.

sincerely,
undecided

FROM THE SOUL OF DANNY

This section contains solo poetry by myself, Danny (D.B. Wright). In selecting these poems, I thought about my connection to Mia and her influences on my writing style. In particular, how she has encouraged fearlessness and freedom in my expression.

"The fears we don't face
become our limits"
-Robin Sharma

Life after Death

I don't know what happens after death
-no one really does -
But I do know it can't be any better
Or worse than this life.
No heavenly promises
Can hold a light to the cherubic hysteria
Of a baby's laughter,
Cackling with innocent joy,
Not comprehending why.
No angel - of any god(s) -
Can hope to achieve such purity.
No corners of hell
Can hold darkness as tightly
As the walls constructed
Around my pain.
No deadly invention
Offers worse intention
Than the crevices of my twisted mind.

What if I were to reincarnate?
I suspect I'd be neither delighted
Nor disturbed
By the outcome destined to me.
Perhaps I'd be a great whale,
Peacefully flowing through oceans,
Yet constantly threatened by cruel men
With horror harpoons
And barbed moral compasses.
Or maybe a lowly mayfly,
Packing life into just one day
But at least free of the burden
Of tomorrow or yesterday.

It's all a matter of perspective;
Death looms heavy to those living 'free'
Whilst those looking over broken shoulders
Often find forwards a hopeless direction.

Risen Reformation

Bubbling from ashes of woven agonies, she rises with
smoke-signaled intent. Scars ripple across charred skin but
pain is a yesterday lament.

Eyes have melted away to become globes of black ink: she
writes her destiny with mere glances: unfolds her story from
slices of dimensional voids.

Hate caked lungs reject temperate air; these mortal organs
rendered useless: superseded by supernatural mechanisms.
Breath is naught but a lost notion.

Hands ripped, and swollen thick, from struggled resistance,
extend and grip with promises to slit insidious carotids.

Still tender violations echo angry convulsions
of divine vengeance: retribution rests on tongue and teeth
ready to release mayhem.

She does not reside in basic planes; soul neither lost nor
found. Her existence instead lifted from words written in
ancient sands.

She seeks no final destination: only the journey matters.
Long forgotten palpitated rhythms punctuate the
predestined path.

Good and evil are irrelevant conceits; jagged rocks of
sufferance and crumbling dust of wrath are the all that
remain.

This is not a rebirth / This is a forging of life and death /
This is reformation.

Bloody truths

I'd rather spill my bloody truths
than hold a gauze against deceit.

Satiate

There's a breath;
Enough to fill a gods chest,
And a sigh
That echoes on distant winds.

There's a hunger
Of a hundred years,
Bubbling rage
Prickling on skin.

Mortal teeth
To ethereal fang,
Heart beats
To demonic drums.

Her repletion
Was almost complete,
Redemption
Via moonlit feast.

She's stalking
Amongst the soppy sheep
Searching
For the prized meat.

Their soft sins
Will not satiate this itch,
Only heinous fluids
Can suffice this.

There's a scent
An antithesis of cologne,

Mind Lesions

Nasal drenched
In target aromas.

There's movement
Quick as lizard licks.
Primordial forces
Hadean instincts.

There's a skirmish
As an egg against a rock.
Devour follows death
Executed in a flash.

There's a quivering
Like oceans birthing birds.
A contentment
Light on dark wings.

There's fatigue
As Autumns leafless trees;
Hibernation
The cycle is complete.

By their name

Today,
Take those crowns
and wings
off your lips
and call your lover
by their name;
not King or Queen,
Goddess or Warrior.

Today,
just call them
by their name.

The Abyss

It drips, the abyss
On to, and into
Everything,
Settling on skin
And old sins,
And it stings
Sorry eyes.

It slips, the abyss
Out of sight
Into thoughts
With naught
In our power
Or persuasion
To stop it.

It ticks, the abyss
Stuttering through time
Like an injured clock
That's long lost
It's rhythm
And reason
To exist.

It sticks, the abyss
To blood, bone
And conscience,
Greedy leeches
Indiscriminately
Draining the
Life from us.

It rips, the abyss
The seams of
Esteem fabric,
And tragic
Memories
Flood in
To focus.

It sinks, the abyss
Into synaptic banks
Of babbling memories
Scrabbling for any
Tiny opportunity
To drown out
Our faiths.

It's onyx, the abyss
A black, lonesome
Mortal pit
Where fits
Of demonic rage
Agitate angels
Calming light.

It licks, the abyss
At old scars
And new bleeds.
Nefarious deeds
Speak seductively
Of false promised
Affections.

It stinks, the abyss

Of haunted things
We've loved but lost.
All the counted costs
Of sinful mistakes
We've made along
The way.

It grips, the abyss
At our chests
And our throats,
Till we choke
On its wishes
And our limbs
Fall submissive.

It spits, the abyss
Bitter little bits
Crackle and pop;
Oily hot rocks
Of self-doubts
And lonely
Ideations.

It tricks, the abyss
Twisted whispers
Echo as screams
Of lost dreams;
Savage nightmares
Pin us down
In sad places.

It sits, the abyss
In sharp crevices
Patiently waiting
Venom baited
To strike at
Our weakest
Moments.

Custody

I'm back to the cheap lipstick.
It doesn't keep my lips moist enough.
They are drying up just like the money has.
He left my life quicker than he'd rip off my panties on
Tuesdays.
Tuesday, that was my day.
His slut on Tuesday, a nobody the rest of the week.
Does it make you feel better knowing I'm tragic?
Do you feel a sense of superiority?
I never felt sorry for you;
I built up an image of you made of all the bullshit he told
me, and all the things I hated about my mother.
Deep down I never believed any of it.
He was a compulsive liar, I know that now.
I know you loved him.
I know you weren't violent.
I didn't think you were crazy,
Not in the way he described.

He screamed your name sometimes while he fucked me.
Right as he exploded inside me he'd yelp out your name.
I don't think knew he did it.
I never said anything.
He never said anything.
If I'm honest, it was kind of hot.
I don't even know why I'm telling you that?
Maybe you'll feel better knowing he thought of you, even
inside of me.
Maybe I'm just being a cruel bitch.
Either way, I don't care who was in his head the most.

I didn't want to own him;
It never felt like a competition.
It felt like... custody.
I got Tuesdays and rare weekends.
God knows what days the others got - you knew there were
others right?
And you, you got what was left.
I was fine with it.
There, I said it: I was fine with the arrangement.
I don't feel scorned or betrayed.
I don't feel embarrassed or ashamed.
I do feel angry:
At me for not feeling,
At him for Dying,
At you for being the name always on the tip of his tongue.

Concrete

You poured concrete down my throat;
a sarcophagus of words,
on which I slowly choke.

A thousand times

I can wear them, if you want:
The clothes that drive you wild.
I can make the make believe faces,
Put on pretty make up,
Smile and curtesy,
A good little patsy,
You just have to ask me.
Just have to want me.

I can do them if you want-
The things she won't do to you;
The things you can't even ask her to.
Things you think are freaky kinks.
Things you think I won't know,
Things you don't know yourself yet,
But I know -
Because I've been here before
A thousand times.

I can pretend if you want,
To love or loath you.
(Spit on or kiss you)
Anything you desire:
A crumbling little miss innocent,
Or an earth quaking mistress of fire.
I can speak in snobby tones
About how I want to be punished and Owned
-Or-
I can speak with feral inflections
About the parts of you I'm going to undress

(Devour / Digest)
And infect
with bitten brutality.

I can say it if you want:
The four letter word on the tips of every tongue.
(And heart beat)
FUCK
Fuck me
FUCK. ME.
I'll even make you believe I mean it.
Believe I actually want it.
(I promise there's not a notion of vomit forming on our
fornication)

I can hate you if you want.
Scoff at every word that falls from your ugly lips -
Point my finger in your filthy mind eyes,
And make you sorry.
Ugly Sorry
Dirty sorry.
Sorry you ever met me.
Sorry you even exist.
I can cause pain that stays for decades
And you'll still thank me,
For what I give, you gladly receive;
Still worship me (with monied prayer)
In the twisted altars of your psyche.
I can be the bitch you wish the sweet ones would be;
The whore they can't even imagine,
And match their innocent smiles while I do it.
I'm the devil in disguise / or an angel in denial.

Allow

Allow my lips
to show you the
missed beats
of my heart.

Tomorrow, Sorrow

Everything sits heavy, like unspent bullets In sniper pockets.
Every breath like adding vinegar to sunburnt skin.
Each thought salts the wounds of the one before it.
A wooden puppet of my inner child sits on my stomach,
drumming on my chest: pulverising my pleural cavity with
the same old beats of near-death defeat.
Each fisted blow triggers new-old visions across my babbling
memory banks.
Boom:

their size.
Bang:

their smell.
Boom:

 their nails on my sickly skin
Bang:

their spittle falling on my face.

Wake, wake, wake: I want to wake up but realise this is a
waking nightmare, not the sleeping kind. Monumented
molestation memories murder my mind. I fail to unsee what
my eyes didn't hide: I fail to seek what I can't find.

Death flashes as the only path to escape.

Violent intentions cause hyper-tension in senses, spilling
emotions in rage to the page. Pill prescriptions drip
complicit deceptions in my drug drained brain.

Vacuumed breaths boil in desperate veins, crippling blood
to a standstill. Languid limbs sign language loss and lament.
Final throes of existence falls on blind eyes and sentience

fades to black silence.

Fighters cannot flee and leaders cannot follow:
Borrow yesterday's agonies to pay for tomorrow's sorrow:
seal each sin with soft kisses and pin virtues to lost wishes.
Don't forget to reminisce, don't neglect what you might
miss.

Exit stage left, return for a final act: life isn't a game it's a
play.

Scorched Lips

I hoped that kissing demons
would scorch your name
from my lips.

If I whisper

If I whisper: I miss you, will you return?
If you bring back your fire, will I burn?

If I whisper

If I whisper: I miss you, will you return?
If you bring back your fire, will I burn?

My Mind

My mind is raining brainstorms.
Mixed up cold front thoughts
of all sorts of poetry porn.
I've had this wild weather
Swirling my cortex
From since I began this existence;
A hurricane of Ideated insistence.
Any form of resistance
(Excuse the Star Trek reference)
Is futile.

They can't rip up my pages
Because my pages are synaptically created
Craze phased phrases,
Delivered in hazy maybes,
love me or hate me,
Anti poetic, off topic, exotic, emphatic
Off beat, of key, non fleek,
Forgive me father
For I have sinned
Style.

They can't take away my pen
because my pen
is only in my head
Scribbling life and death
Polaroid modus moments
So only I can own this.

They can't stop my screen time
because my screen time
is behind my own eyes,

And sometimes
I don't know what rhymes
Will create which lines.
It's all raw and live from mind,
Fresh and unrefined,
Subconsciously derived
From the world wide
Zeitgeist Hive.

I'm a poetic pix and mix box of mystery sugar fixes;
You might get silly string rifts
Of life's fluff with no substance,
Or it could be bon-bon-bombs of harsh truth,
Trauma and abuse,
I really don't get to choose.
Its born as conclusions
Before I even conceive it.

It's my life on vampire tap
Relived with the fingertip taps
On a vacant vacuous vessel;
Evil deceitful devices.
We, wheeled mice
Conditioned to delight
In dopamine fixes.
These little snippets of mysteries;
My bits and pieces
Of joys, hurts, pleasures and stresses.
Unconfined dirty messy,
But pure and unapologetically
Me.
Me.
Me.

Refuge

I chose refuged darkness
Over predatory light;
I accept damnation
over melted candle hope.

Hold it Together

Fear flutters it's feathers
In flightless cages,
And, in stages,
I forget how to fly.
How to write-
How day and night
Should and might
Dance silhouettes
Under sapphire skies,
And I don't know why
It's happening;
The entwining
Of the tethers,
not holding together
And it seems
My dreams
Are tearing at the seams,
As friends and family
Lovingly see
And warn me
But I stay oblivious
For, ignorance is bliss.
Thoughts flitter like glitter
In the high ether
But burn on meeting
Low atmosphere;
An aftermath of embers
Sizzle in my breath
I'm left bereft
Life a listless
side-less, size-less
Colourless mess.

Mind Lesions

The void is unavoidable -
A bottomless pity pit
Cherry picked
To hit
Where it hurts.
Hurt dominates intention -
Love jostles for attention,
As the ashes
Rain down redemption
And I still can't mention
Its name.
The pain.
I still can't name for you this pain.
Monochrome melancholia
Massacres my mind
Leaving behind
Blood Stained remains
Of the day.
Those days
When agony and play
Shared the same space.
And the faces
Of resting bitch relations
Drip like condensation
On cracking conscience;
Synaptic unnatural disasters
Hurricanes twisting grey matter
Monsoons of malicious memories
Leave drowning shapes
In dark head space
Where disgrace meets
With regret and shame
To beat me again.
To beat me insane.

Mind Lesions

To beat the blame
Back into my brain,
And I claim
To be okay,
As acid rain
Corrodes its way
through rusted recollections.
Melted thoughts collecting
In pools of poisoned regret
forgive melts into forget
Sub-conscience spits bubbled nonsense
Until I press reset.

Majesty

Your majesty lies in wild waves
Which wet my timid shores,
In shadows of seasons,
Behind coloured facades,
Where toil and toll
Work non-magic -
Life is returned to life
Over and over.

Pi

What if you plucked out my eyes,
and using Pi,
calculated their radii?
If only you could see
what I have seen
with these eyes -
it's enough to turn a passionate man blind,
or at least turn the other cheek.

Glimpse (dedicated to Mia)

I wish it was possible to rip out these eyes and play back their scenes to you. If you could see the world as I see it for just a moment; you, the mesmerising lead in an otherwise bland reality. You allow your imperfections to noose around your beautiful existence, when you should wear them as badges of hard-fought honour. Apply them like war-paint: Let them glimmer and shine with pride and without prejudice, for those sparkling flaws are you: the you that you are to me.

Give me your lumps and scars: let me kiss and caress them first. Let me read your journey in the bumps and blemishes of your skin. Let me hold your flinches and quivers and still your trembling trust. Allow me to bath in that soul which others only ever see in glimpses and shadows.

Let me pat away your tears with my own cheeks so we share the pain as it falls from your oceanic eyes: our noses clash slightly as I press my face into yours: our hair flickers and dances together as it meets. Let our touching chests syncopate our mourning hearts, to beat together as lovers or warriors. Your tears are my tears: your pain my pain. Your rage and fury boils in my own heart and soul.

Allow the burdening load to fall away from your body as my bones bear your heavy woes. My heat will melt the shame from your pores into mine. Regrets and mistakes dissolve to nothing as our breaths rise and fall in tandem. Cling to me for as long as you need; grip my hands and wrap yourself in me, until you believe in yourself enough to own the world again. Then, let me stand beside you in awe: revel in your grace and majesty. In the blink of an eye ready to burn in fires and die by your side: or pull you to my solace to heal one more time.

A haiku

When there are no words,
And language is not enough,
We laugh, and we cry,

Dance with love

Some people will dance
with your love
But run away
when you ask them to lay
With your pain.

Unsane

Yesterday, I had the strangest feeling
Like all my thoughts were merging
Into one tangible, discernible reality.
Some kind of twisted rationality.

A world where two and two was four
The top was the ceiling, the bottom the floor
Left was left, right - not left - was right
Sunshine was the day, moon was the night.

The sky, correctly up, seemed to be blue
Not twisting hazes or crimson hues
The ground stayed still as I walked
And the trees didn't dance or talk.

The air I breathed was placid and free
Not one lung full causing choke or heave
And the birds circled innocently above
Not whispering secrets about my loves.

The people I meet seem real and indigenous
Not far-fetched fragments or figments
One wishes me a pleasant morning
Which sends my brain fearfully spinning

I felt sick to the stomach at such depravity
I had to take another pill to relax me
There's no way I can further bare this reality
It's all too much, all to very silly!

The pill took its gleeful effect eventually
And I fell back to the comfort of insanity.
Where I could be free with my indigence
And live a blissful life of ignorance.

O

An orgasm
is Mozart
playing Metallica
across your spine.

Demons

Sometimes, even when light is bright,
I see only casted shadows
And the shapes of monsters.
When else the world seems at rest,
I receive visits from unwelcome guests,
Who weigh heavy on my tired chest.
In the most silent hours
Creatures are sent to creep,
And disturb my precious sleep.
Odious, opportunistic imps,
Circle my love-lonely bed,
Seeking asylum in my head.
They attempt to entice me
With their powerful vices,
And sweet toxic devices.
I've fallen so many times
Tricked by false prizes.
Back to my demises.
Yesterday though, I didn't fall;
I squeezed them into a bitter ball,
And hurled them against the wall.
But, relentless and limitless,
They will calmly incubate;
Snicker as they sit and wait.
For the longest of times
I'd been doing more than fine
Sunshine meeting my mind.
But, In the deep crevices of my psyche,
They still loom ever so patiently;
Traps seductively baited.

Barred mind

I try to bend my mind
around all the things
that have hurt me.
It's exhausting setting up
diversions and roadblocks
between my synapses.

The delicacy of my psyche
sits barely stable
in a locked box of memories.

Then you,
you come along;
a crowbar
jarring it all apart.
        Knocking me off sync.

And I sink;
Thoughts slink
Through mind's
eyes and ears,
Germinating fears,
Deconstructing the years,
and tears
Fall down
Ready to drown
Me
all over again.
Each time we meet
I'm sucked back to defeat,
Drenched in anxious alarm
Feeling barred.

Undone

Unstitched
Wounds
Uncut
from skin.

Uncoloured
Bruises
Undelivered
From body.

Unmarked
Blemishes
Unwhipped
From back.

Unstrung
Memories
Unweaved
From psyche.

Untaken
Innocence
Unraped
From a child.

Unimagined
Moments
Unstolen
From dreams.

Unprogrammed
Silence

Unindoctrinated
From sin.

Unshattered
Bones
Unattached
From cartilage.

Unbroken
Promises
Unspoken
From trust.

Unhang
Me
Unrepentant
I
Unremember
It all.

Fads

It's a miracle!
According to the ads ,
A secret the rich and famous
Don't want you to know.
Just a few of these pills,
A blast of this spray,
Six of these chews,
Wash your cares away.
Mix this powder
For a youth giving chowder.
Smother your skin.
Get yourself thin;
Non-fat,
low fat,
high fat,
only fat
Intermittently fast,
Or slow,
who knows.
Perfection awaits you
For a few quid.
But no carbs.
Drink this paste
At quarter paste eight.
Balance your PH.
It's GMO safe.
Look like a rake!

I no longer require eyes to see you;
I know every inch
by heart and fingertip.

Paint Parade

I am made of polychromatic hues
But what colour do you want from me?
What mould and mix fits your filter?
Tell me so I can paint this farcical face
With appropriate joy or tragedy
And fix my fickle features accordingly.

Some colours run faster than others
And some slip from the brush bristles
Dripping neatly at melancholic feet.
Today the easel may accept just yellows,
Tomorrow maybe only the blues.
I can blur and wash them into greens
Combine the best or worst of me.
A compromise to make others happy-
Those who view blues through stained glasses,
Or yellow through heavenly visors.
I choke on the oil of bitter colour combinations
Forced to make accord for correct discourse.

I would rather paint the sky today
And wait a while to paint the sun,
Than splatter mud and greenery
In the places I feel numb.

We place a noose
around our mental health
for a long shot at short wealth.

First words

Innocence is lost:
You can find it under fingernails
Of the beasts who poached it
From me.

I spent my childhood in pain
My teens wondering if it was my fault
My twenties fell aside to drugs and denial,
Hoping intoxication could flush the agony out of me.
My thirties I played therapeutic catch up
Talking myself into deeper nightmares
Trying to reason the pain away.
It never did.
It never will.

Memories were locked in metal cages;
Rusted recollections,
slipping from consciousness.
Words fidgeted on incarcerated tongue
Behind a prison cell made of teeth.

For so long
Fear twisted
Itself around my spine,
Crippling and constricting me
Addling me with agony
Anytime I tried to move forwards.
I learned to exist in stasis
without angering the beast wrapped around me.
I reserved expression
For trauma temper tantrums
And self-harm fits.

Pretty little wrists
And sunless forearms
Tattooed by self-loathing scars.

I screamed a lot:
Into cracked mirrors
Pillows cases
wine glasses
And toilet bowls

I fucked a lot:
Boys with barking mouths
But bite-less souls
Bragging their way into bed
Apologising their way out the door.

I cried a lot:
Under searing showers
Coiled up like a snake
Ready and begging
To shed sinful skin.

I bled a lot:
Pebbles of plasma
Pooling into puddles
Of ravenous red.
The first time I wrote a feeling down
Was with maroon paste;
I let my quivering finger-quill linger
in the bloody sludge ink.
I wrote on to a broken mirror,
"Please kill me"
It was a short poem;
Polite but to the point.

It only got one like.

After that,
The creation floodgates
Burst open-
Tsunamis of traumatic water
Crashing against rocky conscience,
Sculpting jagged stones
Into countless little stories,
Little verses,
Little words,
Of my life.

Cages melted -
Words released
From thought prison.
My mind became a prism
Of repressed expression
Rainbows of pages
Formed by luminous ideation
Catching on howling rains.

Some words charged
Like a rodeo bull
On a furious rampage.
I tried to hang on,
Keep in control,
But the bucks and kicks,
Spins and twists,
We're too much too quick.
It made me physically sick,
Then better after.

Some, like firework displays

Exploding kaleidoscopes
Of blazing lights
Against dark skies
Leaving smoke and silence
In their aftermath.

Trauma was shaken loose
from atop my memory mountain
In aching avalanches.
Decades of rotten remembrance
Surging down slopes
Into piles of compost
Nourishing my truths
Into words and verses.

Some of it sits in the sediment
Of subconscious depths
Waiting for aching extraction.

My mind is simultaneously
A dream factory
And a graveyard,
Where ghosts of dead memories
Haunt the promise of fresh starts.

I can't yet explain this properly
I can't explain myself properly
I can't explain anything,
only write,
Until it's all written out.

Which I hope is never.

Seasonal Upheaval

[collaboration with SueAnn Summers Griessler]

I'm feeling the seasons change
In the soles of my toes and the flow in my veins.
I'm not ready: it's too soon
I'm still in love with spring and summer blooms,
And with you.
I don't want autumn to fall upon us
I quiver at the thought of winters clutch.
I wish we could press pause
And take a few more temperate breaths.

Maybe if I hold your warmth tighter... closer... your leaves
will feel my want.
Stay, please.
I'm not ready to release you yet. I want your arms as my
cashmere, not machinated versions forced on to my skin to
hold on my own heat. Let dragonflies and hummingbirds
cavort a little longer, freeing my smile, not suffocating it
with muddied movements...

We're so caught up in maybe dreams
While the cycle of existence rips at the seams,
Of yesterday, today and tomorrow
There's no time left borrow
Natures laws will lead, not follow.
We must embrace our fate, not wallow in sorrow.

So I'll hold wildflowers in my left hand, snowflakes in my
right,
Balancing heartbeats between the dark and the light.
Finding magic in memories of what was and will be,
Like the changing of seasons inside of me.

FROM BOTH SOULS

So, we arrive at the final section, and the reason for the book existing at all. The following poems were all written collaboratively, as equal partners, about love, life, death, trauma, loss, grief, turmoil, heartbreak, sadness, happiness and everything else that sparked our joint minds.

The collection represents a union of two souls with an unwavering passion for writing, carrying love and truth in our pens.

"No man is an island"
-John Donne

Soul Contract

I read somewhere that souls select the life they lead;
that they know the mortal coil destined to their flesh host
and choose it regardless.

My hand signed on the dotted line and I stepped out into
my field of perception.
Was I consciously aware of my choice?
Did I read the fine print or
did I willingly swallow the loaded gun?
Was I tricked by a higher Self?
Does free will exist or is that a lie we tell ourselves?

My soul must have been a sadomasochist
To pick this pitiful existence,
Or maybe a warrior soul
Took on this challenge
As a test of will and strength.

Am I in love with my given pain and the grief inside my
veins?
Do I enjoy the way it folds me and bends me in half?
Am I craving my impending doom and will I finally breathe
inside my breaking?
Do I rise above it all, as I know nothing but this fight?
Am I strong because I have known how to be weak?
Am I warrior because everyone has given up on me but me?

My soul must have been an empath:
To pick to feel everything all at once with such intense
physical and emotional powers.

To have intuition lead me:
1 path shadow work
1 path painful truths
1 path lust that fxcks so good
Or maybe a narcissist am I
Who is never wrong and only thinks about their selfish
needs.
As I tell you it's all your fault
and shove guilt down your throat, without an ounce of
remorse.
I fake cry and pull the victim card.
The empath pulls the death card and makes necessary
changes.

I'm beginning to realise that maybe
My body-less soul understood a journey has stages,
That moments on a timeline don't define a whole life,
Or a life needn't define an existence,
Anymore than the ticks of a clock can define time.
In that contractual offer before them,
Amongst the infinite selections,
They glimpsed the possibilities within me: within our
conjoined entity
And decided to trust in us and our path
In the knowledge that
The end would be worth the hard means.

Hollow Splintered Bones

The wicked wind howls around my body blanketing my vulnerability and bare shoulders: it's desire to envelope me before stripping me raw and silent. My soles crush the crisp dry leaves in the midday sun and I keep stacking bricks upon my sternum till the unbearable weight crushes me like a pill bug born to such a fate. I laugh when contemplation takes flight like a fire bird without a purpose and I lie and say I'm fine. What a fine liar I am that I crack under the weight of my own hopelessness and hollowed wingspan.

I seek solace in substance-soaked sleep. The dreams I find are like a film of clouded plastic wrapping around me, squeezing out hope and complying my limbs to non-movement. I drift awake to the horrors of non-purposeful reality: chores I let my flesh and bones complete while I remain detached and unattractive. Some other being enquires as to my well-being and my skinsuit responds with, "fine, I'm fine". I see no need to correct it; from its point of view it's telling the truth. It is indeed fine, in the way the skin of an orange can belie the rotten fruit within. Subtle skin contusions offer small clues to the catastrophe concealed inside. The finite surface fineness carries thin fragile finesse: the slightest nudge could bring the entire mannequin crashing down, exposing crystallised delusions within porcelain illusions. Delusions within illusions: skin contusions, concealed chaos.

I dare not dream about the good things because I know such things are stolen breaths that I'll never get back again but I put on a happy face: hug myself brave and jump into my darkened solitude rocking my body back and forth into white noise till I unfurl from my fetal position.

Desecrated Depletion

Decaying remains of a thousand broken boned promises persecute my shattered synapses with frozen phosphorus anger: germinating my sacred sanctum with wanton wishes.

Wishes drift to wisps of cotton memories: beds I shouldn't have lay upon. Beds they chained me to. Beds my mind bends around to protect me. Beds that haunt every sleep.

There's a dream I have: in the dream metal bed frames are piled on top of each other, reaching up beyond crimson hazed clouds. I climb and clamber, claw and scramble the metal mountain. As I ascent, some beds slip away from the pile and spin past me, crashing on the floor below. They scream as they fall; human screams.

The pile becomes a pyre as burning smoke rises below. I inhale the fire, for she is me and I am her. I desperately try to forget the way the past has excavated my bones: stuck it's hands within and rearranged my organs: validated me as hopeless: dissected my mistakes: alphabetized my failures: drained me of my marrow, blood transfusion marriage miscalculated miscommunication miscarriage.

She has made me void of you. She has emptied me and made me whole in one pushed breath as my lungs have accepted her flames. Ashes of my ancestors and our ceremony has begun. I sacrifice myself on your altar.

Wishes wash over me in flames. I have made my bed. I will lay here and let you have your way. Bedsheets of erased moments and yet I long to have time forgive my need to haunt you.

It's me.

Hi, it's me.
Danny.
I'm so sorry!!
I know it's four thirty
But I'm going insane
Mania insane.
Feel like my head is full of little planes
All delivering thoughts to my brain
And where I am it's raining
It sounds like water bombs going off.
Did you see that thing on the news -
The bomb scare in Paris?
Holy shit!
I can't imagine how scary.
I'm scared for them
Crying..
I'm sorry. I'm sorry.
There goes my over-the-top empathy.
Mom used to say I over thought everything
She was right. She was always.
Look at me going on
Forgetting about your mom
Is she getting better?
I hope she is.
I'm crying again.
God, I'm sorry.
Sorry for bothering you so late.
Or early!
I'm such a nightmare
Well, I guess it's daymare, technically at this time.
I'll stop now.
Sorry. I'll pipe down.

It's just. You know.
I know you'll understand because you get like this too.
Well, you said you do.
It was you
Who said you do?
I can't remember now
My brain is frigging fried.
Sorry.

Hi, it's me.
Mia.
I'm not sorry for who I am.
I know it's 3:33 a.m.
I woke up drenched in sweat
My heart pounding out of my chest
My room spinning is a kaleidoscope of broken nightmares
where he rapes me and chokes me from behind till I can't
feel anything but myself falling into
the void
I can't see clearly
I don't know where I am
I feel him inside my every pore
I begin to convulse
I must purge
Release my vomit
Puke you out of my DNA
My brain is firing on all cylinders
Running slipknot slipstream scenarios
Flashing lights in front of my eyes
Oh God I hope the police take you away before I gut you like
the sick fuck you are; rip our baby dreams out of you
I don't fucking love you I say to you
I love you say repeatedly
STOP

STOP
STOP
Fucking saying that to me
I know you don't understand me
You never will
You're done hurting me and I'm done having you molest my
nightmares
Fuck you
Fuck PTSD
Fuck anyone judging me
Am I sorry?
I think the fuck not!!

Sickle Cycle

The demons come and stomp on my chest: concave my ribs: rip out my guts. I am their favorite meal of the day. I scream to a godless god but none of them hear me. I kick and cry and gouge out their eyes but it's too late for me. I know what death feels like all too well. Now I lay here until I am no more.

No more. no more? NO MORE! I will rise and shine, weaponise my Devine, turn time if I have to. I did not retreat, I repleted. I am fasted and ready for blood and flesh against my esophagus. I will feed and feast until the hardness returns to my teeth and bones. Until my tears transform to angry groans. I will reap what you have sown and use it to grow anew: from fresh little roots I will shoot a vengeful bullet through you.

I will vanquish you. Sickle in hand: cut you out of every part of me. Sew myself back up with a strong invisible stitch: no one loves ugly mangled scars even when they say they do. Imperfectly perfect but still breathing, blooming and becoming a better me.
As blood trickles down sickle and twists around wrists, I have sealed the final writ: the parting of skin as departing gift. Cracked wings unravel and unrip: Ripeness returns to my soul. I am not complete but my half is whole.

You swallow bullets and I watch you pretend to end yourself, but I know you'll be back for me at a later date.

Pickled pink pigmented figments of a fermented imagination

She was pretty in pink but could not hide the stink of her diatribe lies. Smiles and bows and fancy clothes can't mask foul odours: can't turn bitter tastes sweet: can't make high pitched whines un-squeak: can't give an icy touch heat.

She was pretty in her noir gilded masked facade. Pretty pursed lips with the bile coming up her thorax. Iceberg heart: steal cold words: swords behind her back always ready to go to war: warrior she is not. Penny for your thoughts is too high of a price.

Shallow is sensory, but depth requires light and energy from places she wouldn't understand in a million lifetimes. Integrity / trust / loyalty come from the teeth, bones and hardened hands of ancestors: and the lineage whispers of wombs within wombs.

She sits with idle soft paws, licking and purring for cause and effect. Adorned in doubt and concealed chaos. A cartoon of a cartoon of her own image.

She twirls in a prayer circus of lost soulless cross and bone decaying deceivers. Banished from their homes by ancestral rights: freed not of their chains: truth their greatest fear.

Bruised Walls

I was never sure if it was love or war, something in between, or nothing at all. I never knew if the blood in our loins ran faster than the blood on the floors: if the floral patterns on wallpaper had been chosen to match my bruises, or the other way around.

I followed all your rules, complied to the letter: but your alphabet chopped and changed with the seasons of the substances we abused. Small doses of me made you challenge my intentions: large doses sent you in to irritated rage. My unfurled wings both fascinated and infuriated you. Each time you clipped them you would yearn for them to grow again. I dreamed that one day they would grow all the way, and you would set me free.

You and I, a match made in heaven until you learned how to make the devil cry. The gods gave up on us: they refused to hear my battle cries. They refused to intervene. If this is love, I never want to love another as long as I wear this skinsuit over my battered internal scars: as bruises disappear and people forget what your fists have done to me. If this is war then I definitely am the loser as I never hit you back. The devil told me to shoot you in the head while you slept with your arm across my breast. The angel told me to cower in a foetal position and protect my head and face. It's too late, you broke me for everyone. They can all try and see what you've left of me. Your fist through doors. The wallpaper splatter with blood and bruises turned to disappearing acts of: I'm sorry I'll never do it again.

I burned loyal for you like a fool. I was strong when you were weak: I held you when you cried. I forgave you one too many times. I grew wings and you chased me with scissors. Out of fear I took a leap of faith and jumped into the abyss. So far away from you. I became resilient. I became free and strong on my own.

The disrespectable death of me

R.E.S.P.E.C.T I know what it means to me - but you, you bent the word around my body like an oiled serpent and squeezed the esteem right from my bones: emptied my traumatised lungs of worthy breaths: until the word crackled and popped in my bowels, and exploded from my throat in venomous, vomitus, vitriol: splattering against the walls of false hope and burning my lips as it dripped to chin and chest. I'd smother myself in a show of counterfeit reverence, broken hands massaging the self-loathing lotion into my damaged skin.

The word flows off of your coiled tongue like turpentine: the sap sits on the corners of your mouth before you lick it with fervour: taste your disrespect and place it back inside yourself with two fingers. I see right through your glasshouse exterior but your internal organs are an affair of defecating distortions smeared across false ideologies. Your virulent hollowness is an echolocation for all attracted to your petrichor dilapidated dotage.

Your permeable intestinal walls turn themselves against you and you lay in your filth. Your asphyxiation: a "cry wolf" to a deaf, world market where you are just a fucking commodity. Barcode on your forehead states you are property. Your worth will never be conceived.

Lights, Camera, Infraction

These horror films never really go away:
The reels are locked In dusty boxes in the darkest corners
of the darkest depths of my mind.
Then, out of nowhere,
a key turns,
a button clicks
And they just -
-play back
And everything falls back
into focus,
And my least favourite movie
Plays out in my head.
The one where I don't end up dead
But wish that I did.
Maybe I'll change that in a sequel.

Even though I've viewed these scenes
On repeat, on repeat,
A hundred thousand times on my brain-screen
I still wince at the bloody bits,
Turn my face from the gore,
Scream at every jump scare,
As if I'm totally unaware,
Of how this movie plays out.
Still I Shiver and slither down my seat in defeat at the dark
corridor chase scenes.
Slap my hands against tear and snot soaked face in
disgrace and shame every time I didn't do anything
wrong.
I bite my fingers as evil lingers around every corner.
I lose command of breath and bladder when they make

their cameo appearance: becoming a dirty little asthmatic
bed-wetter.
I vomit up my guts as they steal the show all over again.
I still hate and hurt myself as the end credits roll, and roll,
and roll.

The reel plays on a Truman Show conveyor belt till it
greets me
face to face inside my day;
kiss, kiss on both cheeks,
tongue kiss my mouth.
'I know you well'
she says.
do I scream about
how much pain I'm in?
do I cry and pretend to forgive myself for all the wrongs
I can't make write: I am out of paper.
I watch till the very end and sigh.
I cannot take my eyes away;
the end has been penned
and still I am
on the edge of my seat
biting my nails-
this is getting so good-
do I get to live this time?
The theatre is empty;
just me sitting criss-cross applesauce.
my demons brush my hair,
slap my cheeks pink.
'you need to hide your tears'
they say,
'it's really not that bad: you're just fucked up in the head'
they spell,

'many little girls had it worse than you: suck it up
buttercup'
she spat.
my memories deleted,
I cannot put my finger
on the correct time
of when I lost my faith
and my innocence.
Some days I still I believe I am
2 pony tails happy again
before I stood in front of the train.
I eat the popcorn and wait
this must have a happily ever after:
if you fool yourself into believing
suchlike things into existence.
I am weak, just a trampled mouse
refusing to die.
I resuscitate myself
and go on with my day like nothing
is wrong.
the movie goes silent,
and I remember this part.
the darkness had consumed me;
mutism till the sun was gone,
and autumn came with my fall.
I want to remember how I lost me:
how many times was it?
was I ever happy or was I born this way?

My existence is either these painful scenes, or the darkness
in between. so, I sit in this pit, slowly falling away until the
next replay catches and tethers me back. This movie is
made of agony but at least I know I'm alive: alive on the
screen but dead behind the scenes.

Vacant Valediction

My blinking eyelids swing over sleepless eyes; vacancy signs in front of empty grey matter. My mind is a room to let; recently empty, previously used and abused. Open to all comers, welcoming to none.

I am not just damaged goods: I am a crash test dummy of shattered happenstances. My goods have been battered and smashed to pieces against angry walls; incinerated in fires of self-loathing.

I want to peel off my skin suit and start again. Wash away the dirt and scars: stand bare and vulnerable in front of the mirror. Do I recognize the real me or is this all an illusion? Do I hear my inner child screaming or is that my lungs throwing themselves against my barbed wire fences?

I am an afterthought of the gods. They don't remember my existence on my birthday or the other holy 364 days. They don't watch my beheading but paint the doors red with my sacrifice. They victimize me from early childhood and brainwash me to ove my abductor and hate my prepubescent loins.

Is any of it real: or am I playing out reels of feels? Even my pain belongs to others: they treat it as a plaything on cruel barbed strings. My traumas reside in empty spaces I've climbed from a thousand times, to be sucked back down the swollen soul rabbit hole, on a demolition cycle proposed by them, signed by my demons. The angels look down broken noses but dare not interfere again.

Sticks and stones have broken my bones, but Stockholm Syndrome slays me, daily. Forces me to replay me: no edits or changes. I jump from frying pan to fire: flesh rejection to fresh desire: truth denier to liar, liar. Addicted to blistering heat, I cast gasoline prophecy: a pyrogenic sadomasochist. The flames, while they last, set me free. In the aftermath of ash I bleed boiled blood and spew up promises I won't keep.

Blinking is derogatory and breathing is rebellious. My eyesight a distance memory. My heart in his fist, squeezed dry and now begging to be satiated by his adulthood. I am but a beggar of love. A condition I suffer with till my 1st moon cycle, years later. The moon has made me a woman but he has already owned me years before. Strangulation my only succession and he my only common denominator.

Throated Motives

"Mr Right", you turned out to be all wrong from the top of your head to the tip of your tippy toe. Now you're just an abscess I touch with sharp tongue. Steady handed splice. Surgically removed. I didn't need you: like Jesus didn't need Judas. Stop praying: you cannot be saved.
Purgatory till your Daddy takes you home to Hell.

I want you out of my mouth: you make my words sour-mixed and wickedly possessive of my throatbox. Salivating Salinger your disappearing act. Stir the pot with your paddle. Fake Black Box your persona. Elixir your prescription to numb the voices in your head: you are already dead. Irrelevant.

A crumbling carcass of your existence de-constructs my confidence: your stinking mauve bones groan in my chest cavity. My words lag out of sync with lips as you constrict my verbiage. I am possessed by your past presence: haunted by hollowed out heart.

Dismemberment of my brain cavity as you burrow your way inside: discarding my memories and burning my home to the ground.

I want to hear the sounds you make when I jump up and down on your face. Your lungs scream my name and your dick wishes it could worship at my altar. Access Denied: "Mr. Wrong". Tie you to your mistress's bed and let her watch you squirm till the maggots eat out your blackout - drunk heart. I got you wet with just the look on my face.

I crave to fill you with fidgeting dread: break open your

arrogant swagger with lashings of leather. Choke you wide and wretch the mess you left inside your malicious mouth hole. Roll your rib bones and play Harpsichord Death March songs to the tune of your stuffed gob muffled screams. Bite the ball gag or I'll feed you my fists. Tell me your lies one more time before you decease.

Fish-hook your gutless guts: pluck and plate them out in front of you. Watch you go in and out of sanity as you eat yourself alive slowly. Beg me for mercy, but I cannot hear you. Your tongue lays on fine china and I drink my champagne in my birthday suit.

Choke Notes

Mirror, mirror
On the floor
Tell me again
I'm an ugly whore.

Spit in my face and slit my name
Into stretched breast tissue.
Hate me as only you can;
As only we dare.

Recast my near death past
Until I crack us open,
Spilling unworthiness in trickles
From lip, to tits, to lips.
Victimise and despise me;
Give me what I deserve.
Give us what we yearn.

Recalibrate my overthinking
sticky notes,
Pressing down firmly,
Feeling the letter letting
release
Gushing itself
into a freer version of
My Self
Drowning into the void,
White noise licking my tongue.

Forget my hollow eyes
Tell me about:
the ways I want to sin

the feeling of you deep within
the way I let you tell me lies
the way I believe
you are a good God.

Pouring
my darkness
onto your mourning marrow,
Licking myself
off of myself.
No mystery here,
your saliva
is my dirtiest direction.
I bite your lip,
Suck your tastebuds
till you erase my name
from your little black book.

I am your bodyguard
I cover all of you with a tight grip
Choking your bliss: I inhale your innocence.
I am not in the right
mindset, but I know you are
the right one right now.
I treat your withdrawal
with my prescription,
Raping my soul,
Feeling the cold,
escaping my homelessness.
Abandon all that I've ever known.
I don't miss you.
I need you to need me.
I need you to make me empty.
to make me whole again.

Silver glass mimic sister please blister your in-affection on to
my sullied sinful skin.
Sacrifice the white dove thoughts
With black blooded crow claws.
Keep me unclean; maligemini queen
Mark me as always yours;
leave your talons inside my lungs.
I breathe you in till I perish
Throw myself on top of you
your heart my favourite tomb.

Purge Cycle

Sometimes the endless emptiness spills into the fake fullness, foaming at the corners of my mouth as I try to speak my truth. I am gutted by empty promises that I do not keep to myself. I convulse at the idea that my best just isn't ever going to be good enough. Splice my diseased remains and look for my lost hope in the innards of my demons.

I use my thoughts like a blackboard, chalking false feelings to the congregated class of whatever year we're currently graduating. Have I learned my lessons? Are my studies my decimation? Declining to answer my souls questions as time passes and I'm left being studious with broken glasses.

I haven't felt since they stole feelings away. I'm not sure I want or need to feel anymore: numbness seems so secure. I blanket myself in the avoidance and comfort brings me riches of complacency. I am well!! I am well. I am well? I am walking in a labyrinth of my Groundhog Day.

Feelings pound my brain. I take a drug to end this morning's slow impending doom rumble. I have a clear vision of what is to come: peacefully waiting for the calm before the ending. I belong to it, even before I surrender. It owns my bones. Licks my wounds with sea salt pinkish oozing remnants. Calls me by his name and I accept his entrapment, as he enters me repeatedly. Call me chaos: call me calm: call me always yours.

Wouldn't a feeling after all this time erupt like Mount Vesuvius, leaving ruinous dust in its aftermath; coating my reality with deathly ash? Coming together for a most happiest of endings.

Follicle Fornication

I ask them to pull my hair the way you did:
To see if they can hurt me worse than you did.
To make you seem weak and foolish.
I beg them to slap my body,
hard,
harder.
To make it hurt.
To make it hurt,
As much as you did.
I point exactly where to bite -
the same sensitive places you liked to own.
I moan;
Maybe they can make me moan
You
out of me.

They can mimic the hurt but not the hate.
Only you and I can hate me that much.

Maybe they can throttle the esteem back into me,
The way you choked it out.
Choked me out.
Choke me out,
Please
From this life.

I ask them to pound your voice out of my hearing:
I must see if I can sing again
without the pain you leave inside of these shards you break
me on.
You push your fingerprints
into my bruises,
dig your hands between

Mind Lesions

my ribs empty spaces.
Choke my exhausted existence
from your memory bank;
tell me lies
that I believe as our truths.
tell me I am your favourite failure:
spank me into a 4.0,
tell me how many imaginary friends
you will rip away from me,
tell them I think they're dumb,
you want to kill Pinocchio
just so you can be the biggest liar there is,
tell me how my taste
makes you beat me more,
tell me that hurting me
will leave you satiated,
tell me you only love me
when I am crying.

I want them to scratch you off my skin.
Claw the retrospective sin.
I want to feel dirty and used,
A source of amusement.
Hear them laugh
At me-
Not with me.
I need to know you weren't the ultimate low;
I need to be taken even lower,
Six feet under
If necessary.
Hate me, end me,
Placate this twisted craving.
End me.
End this.

Dredging Demons

Predatory sunlight slithers into the room via gaps in dirty curtains. I drag my pathetic flesh from wetted sheets and into the beats and bruises of another self-hating day. I wish I could sleep forever: the waking nightmares are too insidious to bear.

They bore themselves deep within, tearing a whole in my heart: alphabetically destroying my existence. The things that are left make me speechless: my voice box devoid of sound. They have made me stuck in unbearable loop circle pain throws. The monsters have made the world cold for my breathing. I am soft like water: rushing to drown my sorrows,
my soul makes rain clouds and I accept my need to give into them.
They take the sheets and wrap them around my neck: never to speak or be heard of again. I break myself against their bedpost and come up empty.

Giving up is not the same as giving in.
I cease to try and erase them from me.
The twisted biology and bones left inside constantly
reminds of their devilled demands.
But I will not succumb to their demonology.
The broken inner child mind will not bend my adult spine.
I relish the relapse falls
So I can strengthen in each rise.
I have risen from my ashes in a continuum of hope
misplaced but never forgotten from my maker.

Apple Pie Lies

Momma used to make this special apple pie.
The kind designed to cover up the lies
after the latest bout of drink-violence.
Sometimes, the pie would fly across the space between
them: rage fuelled dessert ammunition in their Sunday
confrontation.
An American dream coming apart at the seams of the
pastry.

Pappa wasn't a rolling stone
but a preacher man.
He who instilled fear
into every bone
he ever broke on us.
Momma was so full of excuses-
She told us to get on our knees
Pray to the good lord
to fix our daddy,
We just had to believe.
We prayed for our meals;
they were rarely filling,
but Pappa said
Just be grateful for what you have
But he never did work
a 40 hour week
for more than a month or two.
The American dream
was a bleached out
Dairy Queen Blizzard,
the kind where you go to sleep
hungry and hopefully
without bruised ribs.

Every Sunday
I make apple pie.
It never tastes as good as mommas:
Maybe I'm not as grateful
Of the apply goodness
When it doesn't come
At the cost of violence.

Notification Gratification

Do you ever sense the sealed seams splitting -
Threads of stability falling through your hopeless hands?
A tiny crack in your existence shining glints of burning
luminance at your inner-child.
A dam on the edge of breach; just one more drop of fluid
snapping everything loose.

Do you need gorilla glue
to hold your superficial up,
perfectly placed
as not to slip:
for everyone to see your real
and not your Reel?
Needle and thread I sew you up
with a tiny scar:
the world will always remember you
only as broken
like burial ashes floating on the wind.
Every scar under a microscope,
scientist petri dish experiment.
Exodus explorer ready to burst:
no holding back this earthquake
monsoon.

Do you patch over disasters with dopamine plasters?
Stick clicks and likes over screaming nights;
Scrolling for validation, wrapped up in a mummification of
affirmation?
Are you really
feeling pretty
When you look good
On the screen?

Mind Lesions

Does your art
come straight from heart,
Or does it permeate though a pan handled filter -
Looking for fools gold
Before you're too old -
fade away and fold
Wearing young clothes
And an ageless smile?

Is it your voice you've found,
Or another version of theirs?

You steady hold the gun
to your temple,
fake smile plastered
you twist and show your horns.
You play Russian roulette
with likes, f4f, shits and giggles
to wet your pallet.
You pretend to know who you are but have sold your soul
to the highest deceiver.
You make your parents proud
with your need for freedom
of expression,
but deep down
they think you are
an Insta whore.
Tell me again
how much you love
yourself today.

Puppy Love

Which way do you want me?
What version should I bring to the circus ring today?
I can be light and fluffy like the cute ones you never spoke
to at college,
Or wild and full of bedlam like the ones who never spoke to
you.
I've got a pwetty little purr
I can hum into your lap,
Or I can howl at the moon
Baring bloodthirsty teeth.

You want my gentle eyes to love your flaws and overlook
miscommunications of trust not yet earned.
You want me to deep throat your thoughts but you have a
difficult time releasing your Ego into my stomach.
You want me barefoot and pregnant but you yell at me
when I am not wild and reckless.
You love my moans and my roars but cannot handle the
tears you cause me to swallow.

You smother me with romance and ask me to meet your
mother,
Then you shudder me with violence and ask me to fuck your
brother.
I wore the little black dress and drank expensive glasses of
punch,
Then you tear my frock from my skin and punch blood into
my mouth.
Tell me what makes you happy;
Teach me the right lines which don't invoke this cycle of
pain.

I can learn the words to any script which keeps your beast
tame.

Teach me how to keep you loving only me so we can be in
love eternally. I don't want to have to cut you and run: I
need to save us and stay. Staying faithful to you: to us, is my
dream. Don't let go of my hand, don't go out over night:
stay in tonight and show me how you love me.

Tell me I'm pretty

Tell me I'm pretty.
That's what it's all about right -
You offering light to my endless nights
Of loneliness and self-loathing?
I guess you imagine me
(Half-naked presumably)
Weeping and yearning
For your attention:
Holding my phone to the next validation?
In your tantalising vision,
I'm probably holding my hands all wanton,
In places you decide are attractive,
In exchange for your digital affection.
Transactional affirmation;
Your like for my objectification.

Tell me I am smart.
That's how you slide your ink pen down my thighs-
You giving me head so good
I burst across your spoken-word tongue flipping rhythmic
tones.
You fantasize about what this mouth will do
(presumably sucking you dry).
Screaming your name & laying bare
for your undivided attention:
praying hands
beggars are not present:
feed the homeless
I don't hunger or thirst
I wouldn't touch you with a 10ft pole
I would rather swallow a coal
then ever you whole.

Tell me I am everything you have been waiting for
Down on bended knee.
I do not take thee.
I possess all the qualities you adore: but only take for
granted.
You cannot wait to fulfil my desires
(Half-ass your way inward, innards not reached).
Taking my hands to your chest,
Oh how hollow is your soulless cavernous cavity
Full of Loki trickery,
But I am not your muse
I behead your fantasy and bring you don't to reality.

Tell me I'm sexy.
The best you've ever read-
(But will never have)
Tell me my words drop jaws
And turn heads,
Drop panties and wet beds.
Swallow back my stanzas
And suck up my diction.
I hope the resulting erection
Satiates the validation craving.
Keep reading me more,
Even after I'm read raw,
Finish fingering the pages
From preface to happy ending,
But don't stop:
Read me again,
Back to front.
Memorise the words
But you'll never own the book.
Read all the sins across my
palpitating skin: the sheets don't lie.
You and I have committed zero crimes.

Forgive me father

They preach forgiveness:
The ones who yearn to be forgiven.
They nibble their fingernails to little stumps of anxious guilt.
The ones who hang from their
high horses: eating shards of glass from silver spiteful
spoons.

They say grace before each meal:
The ones who made you to beg for morsels whilst their
mouths gorged.
They spit down your throat and ask you to drink their
hypocrisy.
The ones who the underworld use as puppets for their
united front.

They tell you vengeance is sin;
The ones who created vortexes of venom in your mind,
who shook trust from your bones,
And ripped away innocence like a layer of dead skin.

They tell you that cheating is sin
The ones who cum down everyone's throats with poisonous
prose,
who promise loyalty in a monsoons
while keeping the blanket for themselves on higher
grounds,
Leaving you alone in the cold.

They talk of charity;
The ones who offered you around
like a bong at a frat party.
Passed you around evil hands with demonic plans.
They allow you to OD on their

ecstatic calibration,
oiling down your pistons
just to fit themselves inside of you:
fucking you asleep
till you cry,
they muzzle your pain
for their gratification
peeling off your skinsuit
and wearing you for glorification.

They speak of chastity,
The ones who gutted you open before you knew what open
meant.
Who provoked the soaked and soiled beds.
Who made you believe expressing love was an act of
violence.
They who murder spirits
suck you soulless
homeless
and devoid of purpose.

They tell you to be grateful
The ones who made you fragile,
Like a porcelain doll held by its hair,
Twisting your neck
Kissing your mouth open
with their provocative illustrations.
Illusions on fake eyelashes:
swallowed my shallow remnants
of someone whom
you'll never be again.

Voodoo that you do love

The ghost of loving you haunts me every morning:
In the first hazy thoughts as sleep becomes head-pounding
awake.
I feel your thick fingers clutching my thighs
And your beard against my vertebrae.
I smell that beauteous combination of our morning breaths
and last night's lingering love-making;
Your scent all over me and mine all over you.
I hear your sigh-language hinting that you want me again.

I dwell in the knowledge that your love is my sustenance
and I am your only giver,
Our reality smeared across my breasts and I remember all
the ways you had me.
Waking to our collaborative use of tongues and spoken
words lingering
I drip across your stomach making my way up to my
favourite morning affirmation .
You envelop every love line and moan yourself into my
petals till my dew you swallow and your fingerprints stay
bruised on my skin.
I must show you my deepest depths and swallow your
whole: wholeheartedly stroking your soul into mine and
milking your god nectar down into my tummy's walls.

I feel your shadow follow me to the shower:
The needled heat offers no release of you from my skin.
I turn up the settings but your essence is too entrenched in
my epidermis.
The hotter the dial turns, the harder I yearn your hunger for
me.
I try in vain to scrub your aura away,

But feelings of you flock around every follicle I touch.
I can redden my skin but I'm not ready to give in: to give up
your memory.
No soap can remove your stain from my psyche.
I'm a lustful, sinful zombie.
A hot wet mess voodoo doll
Under your abiding spell.

My day's flames slowly rise and I miss the heat that only you
can put inside.
I'm at the red light and feel your fingers sliding in and out of
my skin's thoughts and I know you won't stop till I have
repeatedly released all of myself down your controlling
wrist.
Your nurturing hands stroke my patience with an insatiable
fervour as I give you all of my freedom.
The hold you have on me is my favourite tourniquet and I
tell you to tighten around me like you mean it.

My muscle memory remains in tension at every reflection of
you.
The only relaxant is the quivering releases which switch the
grief off in momentary bliss.
As ecstasy retreats, the desperate need resets and
repeats; the drums of you slow beat through me,
building and growing and throwing shapes of longing,
How long will this sweet torture cycle of slow burn to
crescendo continue?

Forever doesn't seem so bad like this.

Self Disarm

Every time put my hair up, I see endless ugly. Every time I wear my hair down I see shame and blame. I visualise yanking the hair out, patches of bloodied follicles beading on my worthless scalp. I feel your fingers in my hair and I convulse at the thought. You can't hurt me anymore: not as much as I am hurting myself in this moment of throat curdling disgust. I am ugly-beautiful and my shape shifting scares you.

Each time my fingertips touch my own skin I think about turning my fingers inwards, nails becoming claws, and scratching layers away until I reach sinews and tendons, which I play like macabre harp strings. I am inside myself without a second thought: making lyrical creamsicles that scream out my own name. Bite myself to feel the gushing rush: squirt my chaotic tranquillity down my thighs and lick it up because cleanliness is next to godliness.

The way I feel about this face? Each mirror I walk past prompts a fantasy where I'm smashing my fist through glass, and with the shards I chop at my carotid artery. Slice and dice. Make me pretty. Make me like all the rest. Plump injected lips. Plumb inserted breasts. Brains stuck on TikTok fucking for likes. I want to fit into society too. A dressed-up dolly for play: put me on your shelf: add me to your collection of memorabilia.

Whenever someone says my name, I want to bite it off their tongue and spit it in the gutter where it belongs: where I belong. Don't try to tell me different: I know you are just a forked tongue full of lies.

The sound of my own voice makes me wince with mortification. I want to rip the discordant chords out of my throat - muteness seems preferable to the irritating din I hear from this useless mouth hole. I devoid my voicebox and it pleases all my senses that now I can truly go within and convert myself into who I have always been: silenced.

I distract myself, with anything and anyone, just so my mind doesn't have time to wander to the aching memories, or cower in dread at future failures. Have you ever mourned your future?
Have you ever fucked your way into heaven? Have you ever had the devil tell you that your soul makes him cry?

I have ideated a thousand reasons why I should end it all, and a hundred methods how to do it. Still here I sit in this solid chair, in an old house, on sandy foundation waiting for the tide to take me out to sea: so I never have to see the likes of me.

But yeah, I'll just "cheer up sweetheart".

Dreaming Awake

I didn't kill myself today; a great result in my current state of mind. To achieve this success, I put in an under-time shift: Like work but you don't get paid: unless you count sanity as payment. I drank copious amounts of coffee, popped caffeine pills, and I just rode out the night. Ever done that? Stayed awake all night because you're too fucking afraid to sleep: because sleeping means dreaming and dreaming never actually means dreaming. It means nightmares: the deep, dark, dreadful kind: gut wrenching, back bending, screaming and pleading, leaping from the bed drenched in sweat, tears, snot and piss with your heart almost falling from your mouth and your lungs burning fiery reminders of the wind they stole from them. Floodgates release, I cease to exist as anything but sorrow. And I cry: not like sad crying: deep primal oceanic wails like a chorus of a thousand whales mourning the loss of the Mother of Seas. I warble until my throat chokes, my eyes bleed, and my face aches. In that gap where the angst briefly softens, malignant voices creep in and begin to do their wicked things. To whisper to me about why my past must deny me a future. Exhaustion defeats me and I succumb to the voices.

Now I lay me down to sleep, I don't pray the lord my soul to keep: if I die before I wake: I do pray I can run straight into your arms again.
I lay awake in awareness that in the darkest halls of my mind I hear an echo: it is not of a familiar place or sound. I don't deny its existence: I do not dwell in such hollowed parts as laughter is no more: the smiles are erased clean off

and I must stay awake as not to dream ever again. In the morning I wake and I have failed: failed to keep you out of my dreams. I feel the heaviness of your body laying on me: my hands, my lips are permanent marker bled red: you are not breathing and I don't know where the fuck I am anymore. Heaviness sinks me into my pooling mattress and sheets cling to sweat and screams.
I didn't die today: I go on about my robotic consumerism day: making payments to each demon to keep me upright: to make this life look so fucking cookie cutter.

ABOUT THE AUTHORS

M. Hutman (Mia) - Author:

Mia, a name given to a gypsy girl whose home is abandonment, meadows full of wildflower love, haystacks, running brooks and books underlined and fingered. She resides within poetry, darkness, light, love, magick, sarcasm and a heart too misunderstood to be held by gentle hands. She bends, she breaks, she dies in her dreams and nightmares but never chooses to end the continuation because purpose is greater than anything else.

Connect with M. Hutman-
IG: @Glimpsesofmysoul11.11

D.B. Wright (Danny Boy) - Author:

D.B. Wright resides in England, but his heart and soul belong to Ireland. A loving husband and father with a passion for words in all forms. Outside of writing he finds solace and joy in his family and friends, movies, and thoughts of travel. He is committed advocate and ambassador for mental health, working on a volunteer basis to support people with their battles, having battled his own traumas and demons his whole life.

Connect with D.B. Wright-
IG: @d.b.writes
Fb: dannyboywrites

SueAnn Summers Griessler - Cover artist

SueAnn Summers Griessler is an artist and writer from upstate New York. Having discovered the power of the arts to stir emotions within her at a very young age, she knew that this gift was meant to be her career. SueAnn works with a variety of mediums and styles; most of her work is in watercolors or acrylics, graphite mixed with pen and ink. She believes that hope is a superfood; and hate ruins the palate. A mural she painted of the Seabee Memorial while in the military, hangs in Pearl Harbor
Connect with SueAnn-
IG: @the_musing_palette

www.ingramcontent.com/pod-product-compliance
Lightning Source LLC
Chambersburg PA
CBHW031334060726

47590CB00007B/2453